EXTREME LIFE CYCLES

SURINAM TOAD

WRITTEN BY
E.C. ANDREWS

KidHaven
PUBLISHING

Published in 2025 by
KidHaven Publishing, an Imprint of
Greenhaven Publishing, LLC
2544 Clinton St., Buffalo, NY 14224

Written by: E.C. Andrews
Edited by: Rebecca Phillips-Bartlett
Designed by: Amelia Harris

Cataloging-in-Publication Data

Names: Andrews, E.C.
Title: Surinam toad / E.C. Andrews.
Description: Buffalo, New York : KidHaven Publishing, 2025. | Series: Extreme life cycles | Includes glossary and index.
Identifiers: ISBN 9781534547070 (pbk.) | ISBN 9781534547087 (library bound) | ISBN 9781534547094 (ebook)
Subjects: LCSH: Toads--Juvenile literature.
Classification: LCC QL668.E2 A537 2025 | DDC 597.87--dc23

Manufactured in the United States of America

CPSIA compliance information: Batch #CSKH25
For further information contact Greenhaven Publishing LLC at 1-844-317-7404.

Please visit our website, www.greenhavenpublishing.com.
For a free color catalog of all our high-quality books, call toll free 1-844-317-7404 or fax 1-844-317-7405.

Find us on

IMAGE CREDITS

All images are courtesy of Shutterstock.com, unless otherwise specified. With thanks to Getty Images, Thinkstock Photo and iStockphoto. Cover – reptiles4all. Recurring images – ReVelStockArt, Macrovector, Eightshot_Studio, Tartila, Miloje, Kirasolly. 2–3 – reptiles4all. 4–5 – PCH.Vector. 6–7 – Rosa Jay, reptiles4all. 8–9 – JSutton93 CC BY-SA 4.0 via Wikimedia Commons, I, Christophe cag CC BY-SA 3.0 via Wikimedia Commons. 10–11 – Dan Olsen. 12–13 – Dan Olsen, Dein Freund der Baum CC BY-SA 3.0 via Wikimedia Commons. 14–15 – Endeneon, CC BY 3.0 via Wikimedia Commons, Frederick P. Nodder, Public domain, via Wikimedia Commons, Morphart Creation. 16–17 – reptiles4all, Fabio Maffei. 18–19 – reptiles4all, Wisniowy, Public domain via Wikimedia Commons. 20–21 – I, Christophe cag, CC BY-SA 3.0 via Wikimedia Commons, reptiles4all. 22–23 – Rosa Jay, reptiles4all.

CONTENTS

Words that look like this can be found in the glossary on page 24.

WHAT IS A LIFE CYCLE?

All living things grow throughout their lives. As they grow, their bodies change and go through different stages. These stages make up a life cycle.

The longer something lives, the older it gets and eventually, it dies. During their lives, some animals continue their life cycle by having offspring.

WHAT IS A SURINAM TOAD?

A Surinam toad is a type of aquatic animal. They live in calm, slow-moving water. They are often found in rainforest pools. Surinam toads are named after a country in South America called Surinam.

SURINAM TOADS ARE ALSO KNOWN AS STAR-FINGERED TOADS.

SURINAM TOADS CAN HOLD THEIR BREATH FOR UP TO AN HOUR.

Surinam toads are usually a muddy brown or dark green color. These colors blend in with the Surinam toad's environment. This makes it hard for predators to see them, which helps keep them safe.

LAYING THE EGGS

When it is time for Surinam toads to reproduce, the male toad makes a clicking noise by snapping a bone in his throat. This noise travels through the water. The female uses this sound to find the male.

When the female finds the male, she spends hours spinning through water laying hundreds of eggs. The male takes the eggs and fertilizes them. If the eggs are not fertilized, they will not hatch.

CARRYING THE EGGS

Once the male toad has fertilized the eggs, he pushes the eggs onto the female's back. The eggs stick to her back. Over the next few days, holes grow around the eggs.

Then, the female toad's skin grows over the egg-filled holes. This protects the eggs. The female toad carries the fertilized eggs on her back for three to four months.

HATCHING

When they are ready, the eggs hatch under the mother's skin. The offspring start to grow in their mother's back. The mother swims around with growing offspring living under her skin!

While living under their mother's skin, the offspring start to change. They get bigger and start to grow limbs. They are very vulnerable. Living under their mother's skin helps keep them safe from predators.

BACKBREAKING TOADLETS

When the baby toads first emerge, they are called toadlets. After growing under their mother's skin, the toadlets break through her skin. They come out through holes in her back.

TOADLETS WRIGGLING OUT OF THEIR MOTHER'S BACK

When toadlets emerge, they look like very small adult toads. They have already done a lot of growing while living under their mother's skin. The toadlets are ready to start hunting right away.

FIRST MEAL

Newly emerged toadlets are very hungry. However, the mother does not feed them. The toadlets need to hunt for themselves. When they emerge, they instantly start snapping their mouths to find food.

Toadlets will eat whatever they can get their jaws around. They will even eat each other! If a toadlet gets in the way of its brothers and sisters, it is likely to get eaten.

HUNTING

Surinam toads do not have teeth or tongues. They eat very small animals, including fish. Surinam toads have toes on their front limbs that look like stars. This is why they are sometimes called star-fingered toads!

Their star-shaped toes are very sensitive. Surinam toads use them to sense when food is nearby. When food is within reach, they suck it into their mouth.

MOVING ON

Once the toadlets emerge and start to hunt, the female toad no longer needs the pocket-like holes on her back. She loses the skin from her back to get rid of the holes. This is called shedding.

The female Surinam toad does not look after the toadlets. After they have emerged, she swims away and leaves the toadlets to look after themselves. They learn everything about adulthood on their own.

THE CYCLE CARRIES ON

When the mother leaves, she gets ready to have more offspring. Meanwhile, the toadlets will keep hunting. Over time, they will grow from toadlets to fully grown adult toads.

When the toadlets are fully grown, they will start getting ready to have offspring of their own. This allows the life cycle to continue.

GLOSSARY

AQUATIC having to do with water

EMERGE to come out of something

FERTILIZE to make an egg able to grow offspring

HATCH to come out of an egg

LIMB part of the body that can move and bend, such as an arm or leg

OFFSPRING the young of an animal or plant

PREDATOR an animal that hunts other animals for food

REPRODUCE to have offspring

SENSITIVE able to feel very well or strongly

VULNERABLE easy to attack or harm

INDEX